IMAGES
of Sport

MOTHERWELL FOOTBALL CLUB 1886-1999

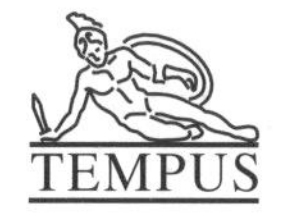

First published 1999

Tempus Publishing Limited
The Mill, Brimscombe Port,
Stroud, Gloucestershire, GL5 2QG

ISBN 0 7524 1511 5

Typesetting and origination by
Tempus Publishing Limited
Printed in Great Britain by
Midway Clark Printing, Wiltshire

This book is dedicated to Motherwell fans everywhere
and to John Boyle for giving them hope.

Colin O'Neil celebrates after scoring a goal against Celtic from thirty-five yards in the semi-final replay of the Scottish Cup. The goal took Motherwell into the 1991 Cup Final which they won 4-3 against Dundee United.

Contents

About the Author

John Swinburne is a lifelong Motherwell supporter. He saw his first game in the early days of the Second World War and immediately became hooked on this Motherwell team that has captured the imagination of thousands of faithful fans down through the years.

An engineer by trade, John worked in the shipyards, factories and steelworks of the central belt of Scotland until 1979. at which point, realising that engineering was virtually dead and that there was little point in chasing the ever-diminishing number of jobs in the steel trade, he began freelance work as a writer.

It was while attending the AGM of Motherwell FC as a minor shareholder that he was invited to Fir Park on a part-time basis by Bill Samuel, then chairman of the club, to act as Press Officer, since the current manager, Ally McLeod, had fallen out with the press and the club was getting very little publicity. As part of his remit, Bill Samuel asked John to compile as much historical information as possible with a view to writing a history of the club for their centenary year in 1986. This took five years to complete, and in 1986 *A History of the Steelmen* was published by Thomas Litho and beacme required reading for Motherwell fans of all ages.

Mainstream Publications then invited John to write an account of the 1991 Cup victory, also well received by the supporters. This meant that 105 years of the club were now on record.

This latest compilation, commissioned by Tempus Publishing Ltd, is a pictorial account of Motherwell Football Club from 1886 to 1999. Over 7,000 photographs were scrutinised before the final selection was chosen and hopefully all those countless players who have been omitted will realise that it would be impossible to cover every aspect of 114 years.

John's favourite games over the fifty-nine years that he has supported the club are (in no particular order): the 4-0 defeat of the Rangers 'Iron Curtain' team on 10 December 1949, the 1952 and 1991 Scottish Cup victories, the 5-2 game at Ibrox, the 4-1 League Cup win at Parkhead in 1950, the tremendous Texaco triuph over Tottenham Hotspur, the Summer Cup victories in 1945 and 1965 and the many games in which the Ancell Babes displayed their talent and artistry before the receptive Motherwell fans, who are, in his opinion, the very salt of the earth.

Since completing this book, John has been invited onto the board of directors at Motherwell FC.

Introduction

For the third time in eighteen years I am embarking upon an attempt to leave some historical knowledge of Motherwell Football Club for posterity. My first attempt covered the history of the club from 1886 to 1986, and this took me five years to compile. The Scottish Cup Victory of 1991, on the other hand, took a mere five weeks to write. This book was entitled *Well Worth the Wait* and it was a personal account of one of the highlights of following Motherwell FC for many years. A pictorial history was a tremendous challenge and I had to rely upon the goodwill of many friends within the photographic world to provide some of the illustrations which will appear in this book.

It is my intention to concentrate more upon the years following the Second World War since this will make the pictures more relevant to many readers, but it is also not my intention to neglect the first sixty years of the club's history completely. There are, after all, some fascinating photographs available that cover this era.

Football evolved in the Motherwell area in the second half of the nineteenth century. Competitions were not yet formalized and teams played challenge matches in which the rules actually varied from game to game. Most of the factories in the area boasted a football team and gradually, as football gained in popularity, matches became more formalized and teams started to play to the rules issued by the SFA.

Most teams were run by committees and eventually it became evident to those with foresight that the way forward was to amalgamate in order to have any impact in the game. In Motherwell the two most successful teams were Glencairn and Wee Alpha, and in 1886 they joined together to form Motherwell Football and Athletic Club. Motherwell played at a number of venues in those early days before moving to Fir Park in 1895. This has been the club's home ever since and generations of 'Well fans have made their regular pilgrimages to this famous old ground to see their favourite team in action

John 'Sailor' Hunter achieved the impossible at Fir Park when he guided his team to the League Championship in the 1931/32 season. For an eight-year spell around this time Motherwell were never out of the top three places in the League – a remarkable achievement. The cup fighting team of the early 1950s were part of another era, and the euphoria of Ancell brought 'Well fans and neutrals alike flocking back to Fir Park.

Over the years many changes have taken place in the fabric of the ground, but the most radical changes were literally forced upon all football clubs by the Taylor Report. This report was brought about in the aftermath of the Bradford and Hillsborough disasters and it was an attempt by the authorities to put right at one fell swoop all the wrongs that had been tolerated by long-suffering football fans all over the country. For too long the revenue generated by our national sport had been taken out of the game for reasons of personal gain, and virtually nothing had been put back for the benefit of supporters.

Under the terms of the Taylor Report, stadia had to be all-seated, thus ending the tradition of terracing which had been in existence since football began. Clubs competing at the highest level were given deadlines to work to and financial incentives to enable them to undertake the crippling burdens of ground reconstruction.

At Motherwell we were very fortunate that the man at the helm was John Chapman. He grasped the enormity of the challenge and set about transforming Fir Park into an all-seated stadium. This was done at a considerable cost and the fans were also required to 'bite the bullet' as these changes meant that there was little or no money available in the coffers to purchase players. John Chapman was aided by a very astute manager, Tommy McLean, who made a major contribution to the club's viability by implementing a successful youth policy. Over and above this, Tommy also had the ability to spot and sign players, often selling them on at a profit. He also succeeded in winning the Scottish Cup after a long wait of thirty-nine years.

John Chapman sold his holding in the club in 1998 to John Boyle, a local entrepreneur, who had made his fortune in the holiday market. After an initial assessment of the existing situation at Fir Park, John appointed Billy Davies as manager following the resignation of Harri Kampman. John revolutionised the pricing structure of Scottish football with his innovative approach to admission prices, while on the field Billy's open and attractive attacking football set about the task of winning back the fans. The 'Inverclyde' methods, introduced by Andy Roxburgh, are still being used to indoctrinate coaches and have only succeeded in driving fans away from football in their tens of thousands. It is like a breath of fresh air to go to Fir Park and see the old values of 'Sailor' Hunter being adopted again. Long may this continue.

Acknowledgements

I have received a huge number of photographs from various sources. Probably the biggest contributor to this collection has been Charlie McBain, who made his archives available to me when I wrote *A History of the Steelmen*. His son Nigel also provided many shots for my second book, '*Well Worth the Wait*. Robert McEwan has been the club's photographer for the past nine years and obviously made a significant contribution, as did Craig Halkett of the Daily Record, whose cooperation is appreciated. Thanks also to the *Evening Times*, the *Motherwell Times*, the *Hamilton Advertiser* and to George Ashton and Graeme Bell.

Many players have passed on some of their own private collection, while relatives of the stars of the past have been very helpful indeed. To all those who have helped me to accumulate the photographs which appear here and have not been singled out, may I apologise, as they really are too numerous to mention.

One

The Early Years 1886-1911

This old print was, according to the original, taken in 1883. It shows the first ever Motherwell team after the amalgamation of Glencairn and Wee Alpha. This match was the first senior game as Motherwell, which they won 3-2 against Hamilton Academicals. The goalscorers were A. Kemp (2) and N. McMaster. Records show that this match was actually played at the original Roman Road ground in 1886. The photograph was later used in 1958 along with a picture of Andy Paton to mark the very first supporter's player of the year award, which went to big Drew.

The Motherwell team of 1886, comprised of the best players from Glencairn and Wee Alpha, are pictured here at their original ground of Roman Road. From left to right, the players are: William Sneddon, Tom Gray, Robert Sharp, James Murray, James Irvine, James Wilson, James Charteris, Tom Sharp, William Moodie, William Charteris and James Cassidy.

The Motherwell team and committee in 1895.

The Motherwell team and committee in 1899. Sadly the names have been largely lost in the mists of time, but some of them, mainly the committee, can be identified from later photographs.

Motherwell won the Lanarkshire Challenge Cup in the 1900/01 season and they are pictured here with the trophy alongside members of the committee. In 1898, in order to give Motherwell some financial help, the SFA had awarded the club with an international against Wales. Around 3,000 cartloads of clay and twelve wagons of ashes were used to raise the terracing, giving Fir Park a capacity of 15,000. A record Motherwell crowd of over 7,000 saw Scotland beat Wales 5-2.

Motherwell Football Club Limited, 1909/1910. From left to right, back row: W.H. Barrie (Secretary), B.W. Gilmour (Director), W. Duffy (Director), T.J. Quirk (Chairman), C. Baillie (Director). Middle row: S. Hill, John Johnston, D. Taylor, T. McDonald, J. Rattray, W. Downie, H. McNeil, A.B. Bowman (Director). Front row: A. Sharp, James Johnston, J. Gray, J. Murray, W. Lawson, J. Robertson, G. Miller (Trainer).

Two

John 'Sailor' Hunter 1911-1946

A young 'Sailor' Hunter can be seen here in his bowler hat on the left of the back row. The goalkeeper, fifth from right in the middle row, is Colin Hampton, who won the Military Medal in the First World War.

The Directors, 1904. From left to right, back row: C. Baillie, A. Bowman, W. White, W. Barrie (Secretary). Front row: J. Fleming (Treasurer), Sgt Major Quirk, A. McLaughlin (Chairman), A. Cuthbertson. Sgt Major Quirk served in the Boer War.

In 1913 W.H. Barrie, who had been the secretary at Motherwell since 1898, decided to emigrate to Australia. The directors presented him with an illuminated address and a suitable 'golden handshake' as it would be called today. Mr Barrie had been very influential in bringing the club through some very difficult times, such as when they became a limited company and also gained promotion to the old First Division in 1904. The high regard in which he was held was reflected by the signatures on his illuminated address. His grandson visited Fir Park a couple of years ago and left a copy at the club. The original has pride of place at his home in Australia.

Colin Hampton became the first Motherwell player to win a cap for the Scottish Football League when he was selected to play in goals against the Irish League in 1912 at Windsor Park in Belfast. By all accounts he had a very good game and only lost a single goal in the 3-1 victory. Colin was transferred to Chelsea on 20 April 1914 for £600, quite a considerable fee in those days. His playing days were interrupted by war and he was to serve as a machine gunner in Mesopotamia. In 1918 his armoured car was shattered by shellfire and Colin was taken prisoner, only to be released with his comrades when the Armistice was declared while being marched to Constantinople. Colin was awarded the Military Medal and after the war returned to playing. His best years with Chelsea were from 1922 to 1924 when he played twenty-eight and twenty-two games in consecutive seasons. He joined Brechin in 1924 but later returned to London to play for Crystal Palace. It is indeed interesting to probe into the careers of some players and I am indebted to Alan Tasker, Colin's grandson, for much of the above information and also the excellent photograph.

A team of former Fir Park stars who played in a charity game against a team from the Motherwell police. The game ended in a 4-4 draw, and was notable for the fact that it was the last appearance in the country of Willie Rankine, who left shortly afterwards to take up a coaching appointment in South Africa. From left to right, back row: Ferrier, Good, Frame, Craig, Newbigging, Patterson, Brown, Walker, McFadyen. Front row: Greenshields, Rankine, Quinn, Reid, Thomson.

A very old and rather tattered photograph of the Motherwell team and officials prior to the 1920/21 season. 'Sailor' Hunter is on the extreme left and it is interesting to see the 'headgear' of officials, which consists of five bowler hats, five soft hats and one cloth cap or 'bunnet' as they were known locally. Their other name was a 'doo-lander.' The players are from left to right, back row: Patterson, Brown, Rundell, Jackson, Stewart. Front row: Dick, Rankin, Ferguson, Gardiner, McDougall, Ferrier.

The tour of South America was organised by a London-based agent. Yes, they even had agents in those far-off days! Mr E. Alcaraz arranged for the team to play a total of eleven games, which would raise £12,800 from this venture – a massive sum of money in 1928. Argentina was their destination and the team eventually returned home with gold medallions, two silver cups, two shields and a tour record of Played 11; Won 6; Drawn 1; Lost 4. The final defeat of 5-0 was by a Brazilian select in Rio in front of a crowd of 40,000. Eighteen years later in 1946 when rationing was still the order of the day and even clothing was by coupon, a large parcel arrived at Fir Park for the attention of John Hunter. When he opened it he found a complete set of claret and amber jerseys, compliments of the Argentine Football Authorities. The only problem was they had reversed the colour scheme and it looked very strange indeed. This strip was allocated to the reserve team who played in it for a full season. This photograph shows the whole party aboard the *Almanzora*. From left to right, back row: Mrs Hunter, Mr A. Donaldson, W. Frame, H. McNeil, R. Little, W. McFadyen, Arnott Craig, A. McClory, D. Thackery, Alan Craig, W. Tennant, J. Johnman, W. Walker, John 'Sailor' Hunter. Front row: George Stevenson, T. Douglas, T. Tennant, R. Ferrier, J. Keenan, J. Cameron, A. McMurtie, Master J. Hunter. The South American Tour was a truly pioneering venture and it was a great financial success. This in conjunction with their Spanish tour gave 'Sailor' Hunter the money to plunder the old Intermediate League which was on the point of folding, and thus enabling him to obtain the backbone of his great championship side of 1931/32.

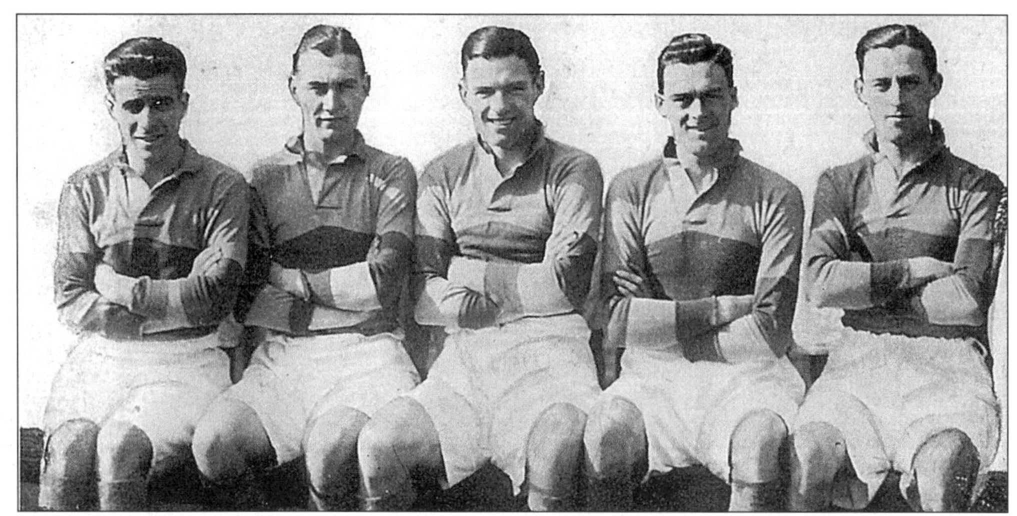

The 'Famous Five' – Murdoch, McMenemy, McFadyen, Ferrier (outside left) and Stevenson (inside left). Their League-winning statistics in 1931/32 were: Played 38; Won 30; Drawn 6; Lost 2; Goals for 119; Goals against 31; Points 66. Rangers were runners-up with 61 points and Celtic finished third with 48 points.

Chairman Tom Ormiston CBE, MP, stands proudly beside his wife as she unfurls the Championship Winners' Flag for the 1931/32 season. Their daughter Muriel is in the foreground.

The Motherwell team which won the 1931/32 Scottish First Division Championship. From left to right, back row: Tommy McKenzie, Hugh Wales, Willie Telfer, James Mackrell, Ben Ellis. Middle row: Andrew Donaldson, John Johnman, Willie Dowall, Alan McClory, Allan Craig, John Blair, Willie Walker. Front row: John Murdoch, Willie Moffat, John McMenemy, Bobby Ferrier, Willie McFadyen, George Stevenson.

The 1930/31 Motherwell team who came so close to victory in the 1931 Scottish Cup Final. They drew the first game against Celtic 2-2 after being two goals up. This game will always be known as the Allan Craig final due to the own goal that he scored in injury time. The gate money received by each team was £1,958 14s 2d. Celtic won the replay 4-2 and Motherwell received £1,871 7s 4d.

Left: Hughie Wales, the dynamic and cultured right half in the League Championship side of 1931/32. *Right:* Willie Telfer, an outstanding left half in the League Championship side of 1931/32.

A composite photograph of the 1933 Scottish Cup Final squad.

The team and officials in full formal wear on board ship for South Africa in 1934 for their second tour of that country.

A snap of the team in Pretoria. From left to right, back row: Blair, Telfer, McClory, Allan, McKenzie, Ellis. Front row: Ogilvie, McMenemy, McFadyen, Stevenson, Stewart, 'Big Wull' Walker (Trainer).

The squad which toured South Africa in 1934. From left to right, back row: J. Crapnell, J. Johnston, T. McKenzie, T. Crawley, A. Hemmings (South Africa Manager), W. Stewart. Middle row: R. Smithers, G. Stevenson, H. Wales, A. McClory, J. Blair, W. Telfer, B. Ellis, W. Walker. Front row: J. McMenemy, A. Muirhead, R. Ferrier, J. Hunter, W. McFadyen. Seated on ground, W. Allan and D. Ogilvie.

The Motherwell team of 1933/34. From left to right, back row: Wylie, Crapnell, Wales, Blair, McClory, Telfer, Johnstone, Ellis. Front row: Dowall, McMenemy, McFadyen, Ferrier, Stevenson, Ogilvie, McKenzie.

Pre-war training took place at a more leisurely pace.

Wales, McKenzie, Stewart and Ferrier put in some relaxing ball work. Going by this it looks like it was Stewart who atc all the pies!

Hughie Ferguson was one of the most prolific goalscorers in the history of Scottish football. He played for Motherwell Hearts and Parkhead Juniors before signing for Motherwell in 1916. In the next nine seasons he scored a remarkable total of 282 League goals, and finished his career with around 360 senior goals. 77 of Hughie's goals were for Cardiff City, and he captured immortality when he scored the goal that took the FA Cup out of England in 1927 for the one and only time. In 1920/21 he set a record of League goals in a season when he scored 42, a total that was eventually passed eleven years later by Motherwell's Willie McFadyen who scored 52 goals in a single season, a record that has never been broken. After his triumphs down South, 'Fergie' returned briefly to Scotland, and he turned out for Dundee where he only scored two goals before his death in tragic circumstances while still only in his early thirties.

Tommy McKenzie served Motherwell Football Club for thirty-eight years as a player, coach and trainer. His brother Willie McKenzie also served Motherwell as a trainer for many years.

This training shot was taken in March 1933 and shows, from left to right: Ben Ellis, John Blair, George Stevenson, Tom Wylie and Bobby Ferrier.

Big Alan McClory relaxes with Wull Walker while the others are pounding around the park. Training was certainly a bit more laid back in the 1930s!

Just before war broke out, 'Sailor ' Hunter gave some advice to his players. They were told: 'If you don't want to go to war then the best thing that you can do is to join the Territorials. This will allow you to do your national service, but also give you plenty time for training and playing football.' These four took his advice, but when war did break out they were among the very first to go. On the left of the photograph is winger Joe Johnstone, and second from the right is Davie Mathie, that hardest of tough players.

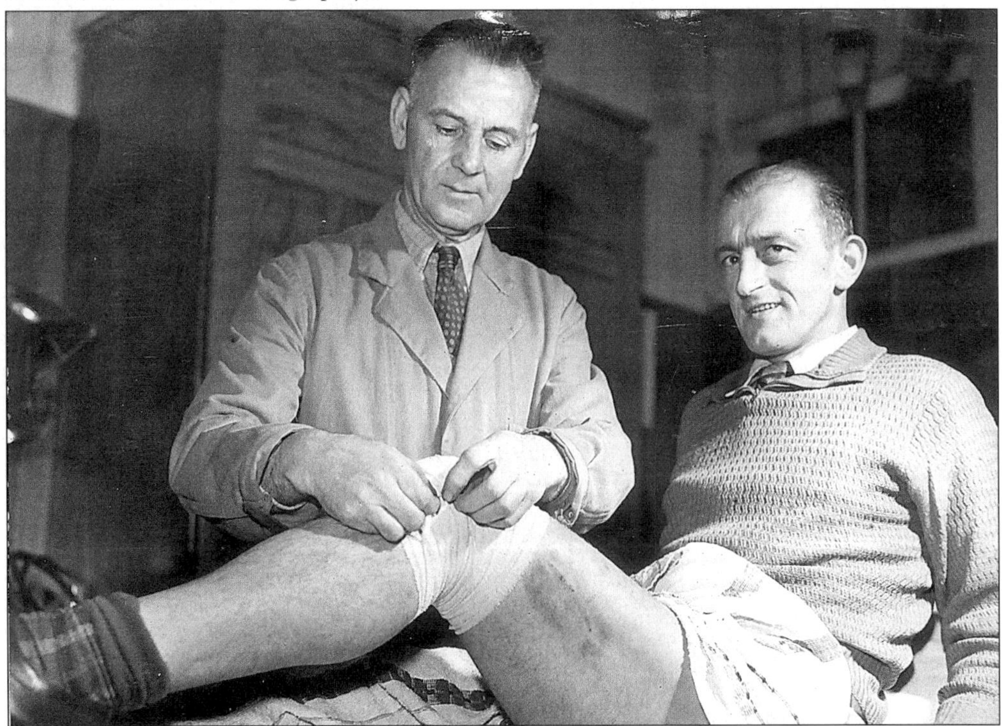

Tommy McKenzie, who was a star wing half for the club in the early 1930s, has now taken over as trainer/physio. Here he is seen giving treatment to Archie 'Baldy' Shaw.

Kilmarnock and Shaw. Willie Kilmarnock signed for Motherwell in 1938, and four years later 'Sailor' Hunter brought Archie Shaw to Fir Park from Wishaw Juniors. This started up a full-back partnership, Willie played right-back and Archie took everything above the grass from the left-back position, which was to last for an incredible thirteen seasons. It is doubtful if this record will ever be beaten, particularly since the inception of the Bosman Ruling, which has given players freedom of contract. The patrnership finally broke up when Bobby Ancell sold Willie Kilmarnock to Airdrie in 1956.

Ben Ellis with one of his many caps for Wales. Ben was rated as one of the finest left-backs ever to play in Scotland and, according to those fortunate enough to see him play, he could head a ball further than most modern full-backs can kick it (or even trap it!).

Three
The Great Cup Fighters 1946-1955

This picture typifies the cup-fighting spirit of the early 1950s team. They are seen here with the League Cup in 1950 after 'trouncing' Hibernian 3-0 with goals from Archie Kelly, Jim Forrest and Willie Watters.

George Stevenson was appointed manager in 1946 after a long and illustrious career as a player at Fir Park. He played at inside left and it is worth noting that one of his contemporaries was Bob McPhail of Rangers, who also played in the inside left position. When both were selected to play together for Scotland, it was always George who was asked to occupy the inside right berth in the team. George had a highly successful ten years as manager, during which his team won the League Cup in 1950 and, of course, the Scottish Cup in 1952. In 1947 Motherwell played the longest match in Scottish football history when they were eventually beaten by Hibernian in the Scottish Cup Semi-final after 62 minutes of extra time. The winning goal was scored by Hugh Howie of Hibs in the 152nd minute of the game. George was also in charge in 1951 when Motherwell lost 1-0 to Celtic in the Scottish Cup Final.

The League Cup Final programme – Motherwell *v.* Hibernian, 28 October 1950.

The Scottish Cup Final programme – Dundee *v.* Motherwell, 19 April 1952.

Motherwell played Hibernian in the League Cup Final on 28 October 1950. The Hibs side were sweeping all in front of them at that time and were the current League Champions. They boasted the most famous ever front five in Scottish football – Smith, Johnstone, Reilly, Turnbull and Ormand, and were odds on favourites to beat Motherwell in this match, only to be thoroughly beaten 3-0 by the 'Steelman' on the day. The headlines in the papers at that time were all about missing nuclear scientists and the following cartoon by Jack Lindsay appeared in his regular spot on the Monday after Motherwell had humiliated Hibs. The Motherwell team in this final was: Johnstone, Kilmarnock, Shaw, McLeod, Paton (Captain), Redpath, Watters, Forrest, Kelly, Watson, Aitkenhead. The goals were scored by Archie Kelly, Jim Forrest and Willie Watters.

The 1950 League Cup winning team with the club officials. From left to right, back row: J. Collins, A. Hepburn, T. Baird, J. Kerr, J.M. Muirhead. Middle row: J. Marshall, W. Walker, W. Kilmarnock, D. McLeod, J. Johnston, A. Shaw, W. Redpath, B. Ellis, J.Hunter. Front row: G. Stevenson (Manager), W. Watters, J. Forrest, A. Paton (Captain), A. Kelly, J. Aitkenhead, A. McNay (Chairman).

The 1952 Scottish Cup winning team with the club officials. From left to right, back row: J. Collins, A.J. Hepburn, A. McNay (Chairman), T. Baird, J. Marshall, J. Maxwell Muirhead (all Directors). Middle row: W. Walker (Trainer), W. Kilmarnock, C. Cox, AA. Paton, J. Johnston, W. Redpath, A. Shaw, B. Ellis (Coach). Front row: G. Stevenson (Manager), T. Sloan, W. Humphries, A. Kelly, J. Watson, J. Aitkenhead, J. Hunter (Secretary).

A proud Willie Kilmarnock holds the Scottish Cup aloft as the team bus inches its way through the mass of fans at Motherwell Cross.

Captain Willie Kilmarnock holds the Cup as he is lifted shoulder high by Andy Paton. Also in the picture are, from left to right: Charlie Cox, J. Collins (Director), Tommy Sloan, Ben Ellis, Archie Shaw and Johnnie Aitkenhead.

The goalscorers in the 1952 Scottish Cup Final – Willie Redpath, Wilson Humphries, Jimmy Watson and Archie Kelly, fill the Scottish Cup to celebrate their memorable victory over Dundee by four goals to nil.

Old 'Sailor' Hunter toasts the team's victory with a sip of champagne from the Cup as Johnny Johnston, Jimmy Watson, Charlie Cox, Wilson Humphries, Archie Shaw and Willie Kilmarnock smilingly look on.

Jimmy Watson's header hits the woodwork in the 1952 Scottish Cup Final.

In the 1952 Cup Final, Johnnie Aitkenhead takes a tumble and Archie Kelly appeals for a penalty. Just look at that crowd in the background! There were over 136,000 fans at this final.

The Directors of Motherwell FC and manager George Stevenson as they left the cinema in Wishaw after watching the film of the 1952 Cup Final victory over Dundee. It is amazing how social habits have changed – the whole of the front row are smoking!

Wull Walker, who had waited a lifetime to see Motherwell win the Scottish Cup. Wull had been trainer when the team had won the League Championship, and he was still serving in that capacity when they finally lifted the Cup at (including replays) their sixth attempt.

The skills of Johnnie Aitkenhead were a joy to behold. The 'wee man' played the game at walking pace and he was a master when it came to dribbling the ball past any opponent. He was the most accurate player at crossing a ball that I have ever seen, including the great Davie Cooper. The 'Daddler', as he was affectionately known by the 'Well fans, was also the finest and most deadly penalty expert that has ever graced Fir Park. For a seven-year spell he never failed to score from a spot kick with Motherwell and simply dipped his shoulder as he went up to the ball and coolly slotted it inside the opposing keeper's right hand post. Jim Forrest scored 28 goals one season, and Johnnie said that he just hit the ball into the net off the big man's head. On 10 December 1949, Johnnie gave big George Young the biggest roasting of his illustrious career, and the 'Daddler' even invented new ways to beat an opponent that day, turning the Ibrox giant inside out and outside in as he tormented him unmercifully. On that memorable day Motherwell beat Rangers 4-0 and 'Big Corky' admitted years later that this game was his biggest ever nightmare.

In 1952 the Lord Provost of Glasgow hosted a benefit game at Firhill with the proceeds going to the dependants of a Constable McLeod. The Glasgow policeman had been killed whilst on duty, and the provost organised a game between the League Champions, Hibs, and the Scottish Cup Winners, Motherwell. The final outcome of the match was a 5-1 victory for Motherwell, and the trophy is still on display in the Boardroom.

Here is a team of 'old crocks' in the 1970s who turned out in another benefit game. From left to right, back row: Bert McCann, Willie McSeveney, Hastie Weir, Andy Paton, Bobby Howatt, Bobby Caldwell (Queens Park), Bobby Shearer (Rangers). Front row: Eric Caldow (Rangers), Willie Fernie (Celtic), 'Baldy' Shaw, Willie Telfer (St Mirren and Rangers), Willie Redpath, -?-.

The 1950 League Cup Winners proudly show off the trophy at the Civic Reception in the Motherwell Town Hall

Football players are continually turning out for charity matches, even although their playing days are well behind them. Here is an 'old crocks' team with three 'Well former players – Bobby Watson, Billy Reid and Sammy Reid. From left to right, back row: Watson, Sneddon, Telfer, Kerr, Millar and Smith. Front row: Cummings, Campbell, B. Reid, Bryce, S. Reid.

This is a typical Motherwell team of 1954/55 and the line up is, from left to right: McIntyre, Kilmarnock, Shaw, Cox, Mason, Redpath, Hunter, Aitken, McSeveney, Humphries, Williams.

Left: Jackie Hunter was a prolific goalscorer for Motherwell in the early fifties. He scored four goals in the club's record victory when Dundee United were beaten 12-1. Bert McCann was playing for Dundee United on that famous occasion. Bert later moved to Queens Park before signing for Bobby Ancell at Fir Park. *Right*: Ian Gardiner was signed in 1955 by George Stevenson. His previous team had been East Fife where he had playmates such as 'Legs' Fleming and Alan Brown. Ian scored a total of 45 League goals in his three years at Fir Park and was also capped while playing for Motherwell. He was probably one of the last of that old style of centre forward who scored most of his goals from outwith the penalty box. He had a phenomenal shot, as did his former team-mate in his East Fife days, 'Legs' Fleming. Sadly, this is one art that has virtually disappeared from our modern game in Scotland.

The first ever player to be voted as Motherwell 'Player of the Year' was Andrew Paton. This was in his final season at Fir Park, in 1958, after sixteen years of loyal service. Andrew was, in my opinion, the finest post-war player to grace the claret and amber, and he played the game to entertain. He was a centre half in the days when they declined the need for sweepers, and he was the hardest tackling defender I have ever enjoyed watching. His anticipation bordered on the clairvoyant and his distribution was superb. Andrew could also be, if provoked, a thoroughly aggressive player, and would have made that modern hard man Vinnie Jones look like a choirboy by comparison! He never shook hands at the end of any match after he was given a severe head-butt by Hugh Brown of Partick Thistle at the end of a game at Firhill. He loved to play against the Old Firm and took no prisoners in these matches. Big Drew was a 'one off' and we will never see his likes again on any football pitch.

Four

The Ancell Era 1955-1965

Bobby Ancell was manager of Motherwell from 1955 to 1965, a time in which he was responsible for changing the entire face of Scottish football. Bobby was to sign a host of extremely talented young players, many of whom were honoured by their country. He was a football purist who once said to me that, 'The delight and feeling of euphoria which we all experienced in the dressing room at half time after scoring nine goals in forty-five minutes was one of the highlights of my career. In that first half against Falkirk I have never seen a better exhibition of pure flowing football.'

Ian St. John in typical pose as he salutes another goal for the Ancell Babes. Note the original floodlights in the background.

Pat Quinn, second from the left, leads some of the Ancell Babes in training. Billy Reid is on the extreme right.

The gales on 10 January 1958 blew away the roof of the East Enclosure, and with it went most of the club's floodlighting system.

This photograph was taken twenty-four years later in 1982. Little has changed except the new floodlights and segregation fence to keep rival fans apart. Advertising is now in evidence, and the terracing steps are concrete. Surveillance cameras are also in place to keep an ever-vigilant eye on anyone whose conduct may give cause for concern.

Sammy Reid receiving a winner's trophy for a yet another outstanding display of five-a-side football. The squad of Ian St. John, Willie Hunter, Bobby Roberts, Sammy Reid and Pat Quinn were unbeaten over a three-year period.

Motherwell had four players capped for this under-23 international match against England. The score finished at 4-4, Ian St. John scoring one and Dennis Law scoring three for Scotland. Jimmy Greaves scored all four of England's goals. The 'Well players are, from left to right: Willie Hunter, Andy Weir, John Martin and Ian St. John.

Andy Weir was, in the opinion of his fellow Ancell Babes, 'the pick of the bunch.' He played his first match at Fir Park for the reserve team on Christmas Day 1957 with John Martis, who I also believe made his debut. They were both quickly promoted to the first team and their careers really took off. Sadly, Andy was severely injured a few years later in a clash of heads with Lewis of Third Lanark, finishing up at death's door in hospital. He was eventually diagnosed with meningitis, and despite overcoming the disease and making a comeback, he never managed to scale the heights he had earlier in his career. Andy at his peak was the most dynamic outside left I have ever seen at Fir Park. He could shoot with both feet and was a real 'player's player.' Unfortunately, Andy died in his early fifties, suffering ill health for some years before his death. The VP Club had a testimonial year for Andy in 1992, and at the Sportman's Dinner in the Civic Centre they handed over a very substantial cheque to him, which he gratefully accepted. Tragically, he died within a week of this event.

When the Andy Weir Committee organised a benefit year for him in 1992, one of the first things they did was to purchase an electric wheelchair for him. This was presented to Mrs Weir on 2 May 1992 by John Martis. John is seen here with several former Motherwell players and some of the benefit committee.

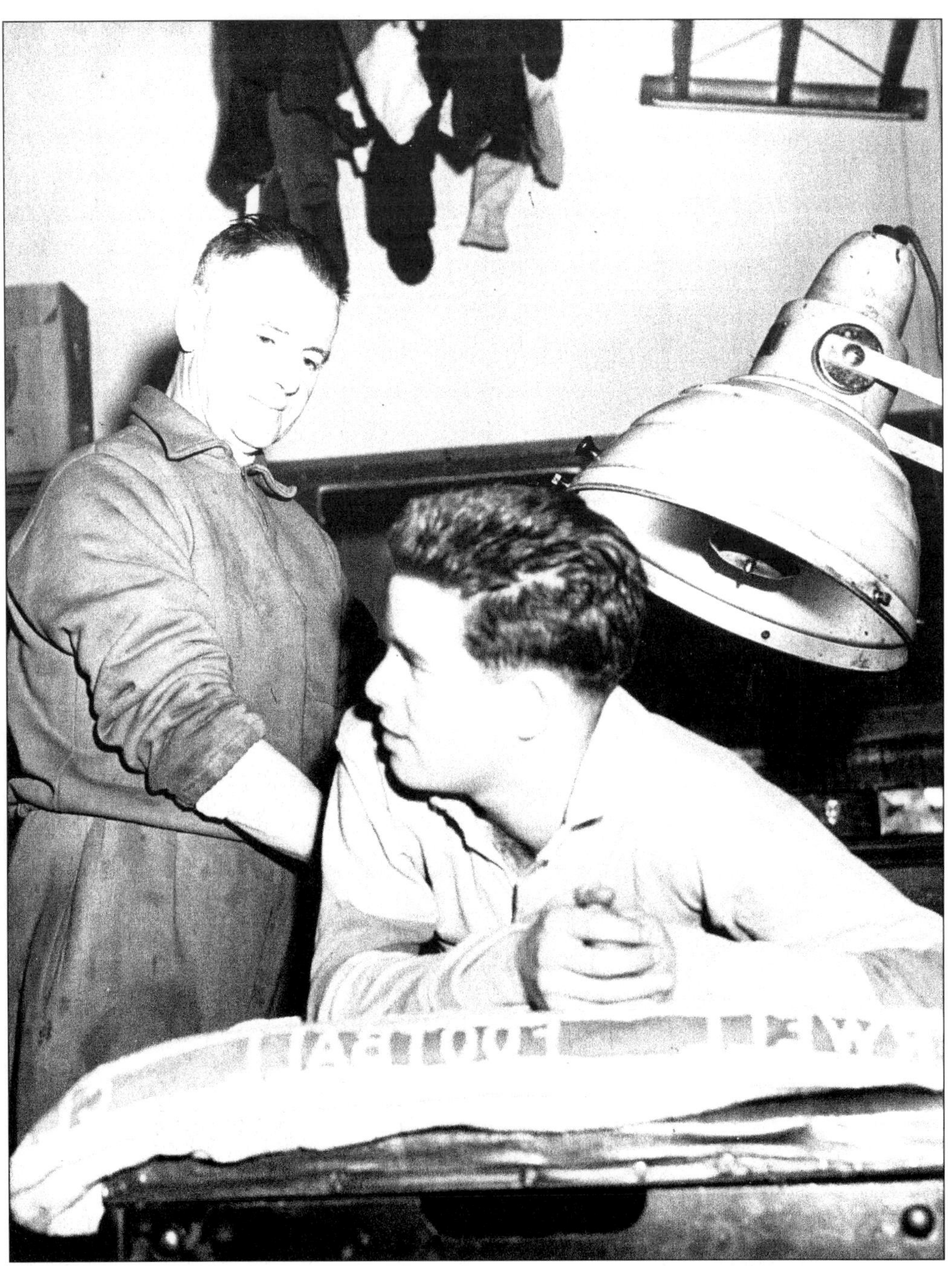

Sammy Reid receiving treatment from Tommy McKenzie. Motherwell Football Club have a very strong and thriving former players club. Sammy is a member of the committee who run the club, as is his good friend John Martis, who became chairman of the FPs after the death of Wilson Humphries. John says this is a typical picture of Sammy at training. Sammy will always be remembered for scoring the only goal of the game when Berwick Rangers knocked Glasgow Rangers out of the Scottish Cup. Sammy's captain, manager and goalkeeper that day was the late Jock Wallace, who managed Motherwell from 1982 to 1983.

Left: John Martis was the player who made such a great job of filling Andy Paton's shoes at Fir Park. It was a hard act to follow, but John managed it without too much problem! John was a great centre half and he won numerous Under-23 caps and a full cap for his country against Wales. *Right:* Jock Wallace was manager at Fir Park in the 1982/83, before returning to Ibrox in the early part of the following season. Jock was a hard taskmaster but had the ability to imbue people with a sense of loyalty. His record in football speaks for itself.

The Ancell Babes in 1958. Note the youthful Ian St. John beside old 'Sailor' Hunter.

The Ancell Babes in 1961. The talented players in this squad included Bert McCann, Andy Weir, Pat Quinn, Willie Hunter, Ian Thompson, Charlie Aitken, John McPhee, Bobby McCallum, Matt Thomson, Bobby Roberts, Willie McCallum, Willie McSeveney, George Murray, Alan Wylie, Pat Delaney and John Martis. That is only sixteen of the above squad who had lost Ian St. John to Liverpool in the previous season.

The structure of the new main stand arising from the old stand. This photograph was taken on 22 March 1962 and highlights the foreshortened nature of the stand. This was due to the fact that if it had covered the full length of the pitch, it would have overshadowed the garden behind it, and the occupants of the house in Fir Park could not come to terms with the club regarding compensation. Rather than be held to ransom, the directors decided upon a shorter version.

Three of the Ancell squad in training. From left to right, they are Charlie Aitken, Pat Quinn and Pat Delaney. Charlie Aitken played originally as an inside right but later was converted to the right half position. The highly popular Charlie became one of the finest wing halves in the country, and had he been playing with either of the Old Firm teams he would have amassed a large number of caps for Scotland. Pat Quinn was one of the most astute inside men ever to 'don' the claret and amber. He played for Scotland and eventually was sold to Blackpool for £40,000 – another big fee in the 1960s. Pat Delaney will always be remembered by 'Well fans for the glorious free kick which nearly burst the net in the Scottish Cup replay at Ibrox. That great goal set Motherwell up for a famous 5-2 victory over Rangers.

1964/65 and this squad included some new players such as Joe McBride, Hastie Weir, Dougie Hope, Peter McCloy, John Moore and Tommy Coakley. Willie Gallacher and Bobby Ramsey are added to the other familiar faces.

Joe McBride was the man who eased the pain for the 'Well fans when they lost Ian St. John to Liverpool. Joe was an entirely different type of striker from 'Sinji', or perhaps I should really say centre forward, because that's what they both were. So prolific was Joe McBride that the late Jock Stein recognised his outstanding ability, stealing him from Motherwell for a miserable £17,500. At Celtic, he played in their great 1966/67 season and finished up as Scotland's top scorer despite being injured from Christmas until the end of that season. My favourite memory of Joe McBride at Fir Park was a hat-trick he scored in a famous 3-3 draw with Hearts. A very strong and bustling striker with a great shot in both feet and exceptionally strong in the air when heading the ball, Joe would have finished up a multi-millionaire if he had been playing in the modern game.

This is a representative of the players selected by Bobby Ancell in his final season as manager. From left to right, back row: Bert McCann, Pat Delaney, Alan Wylie, Bobby McCallum, John Martis, George Murray. Front row: Tommy Coakley, George Lindsay, Joe McBride, Andy Weir, Willie Hunter, Craig Bailey. Ancell had a brief spell at Dundee as their manager but never again reached the level of success and acclaim he had enjoyed at Motherwell.

Matt Thomson was signed as a right-back by Bobby Ancell, although he was also equally comfortable at left-back, centre half or indeed any of the midfield positions. He later became team captain, founded Thomson Litho, and is now one of Scotland's most successful businessmen. Not bad for a former footballer! Over the years he has employed many of his former team-mates and contemporaries to help them make that transition from playing football to real life. Among them were Alex Ferguson, now manager of Manchester United, and Dixie Deans of Motherwell and Celtic, who both played for the Thomson Litho Works team. Matt tells a 'nice wee story' about the day that Fergie nearly lifted the door to Matt's office off its hinges when he found out that Dixie was replacing him at centre forward and that he (Fergie) had to play on the wing. Even in those days Alex had his own ideas about football, but he came off second best to Matt on that occasion!

Matt Thomson and Willie McCallum presenting a trophy at Knowetop School in 1965.

Five

Eight Managers 1965-1984

Motherwell Football Club, 1969. From left to right, back row: J. Wark, J. Goldthorpe, D. Currie, K. MacRae, T. Forsyth, P. McCloy, W. McCallum, R. Campbell, J. Murray. Front row: D. Whiteford, J. Wilson, T. Donnelly, J. Deans, J. McInally, J. Muir.

The irrepressible John 'Dixie' Deans was a prolific goalscorer with Motherwell and later Celtic. Dixie was always in trouble with referees and joked that he used to carry a spare red card for himself in case they ever got caught short. Dixie had that unique talent that allowed him to jump for a high ball and then just hang there waiting for it – for his size he was tremendous in the air. Dixie Deans was truly one of footballs genuine characters.

Bobby Howitt was Motherwell manager from 1965 to 1973. Bobby was the manager who signed Joe Wark, Dixie Deans and Willie Pettigrew among others. His greatest achievement came early at Fir Park when he guided Motherwell to success in the 1965 Summer Cup.

The victorious Motherwell team which won the Summer Cup against Dundee United in 1965 in the two-legged Final. Pat Delaney is seen holding the Summer Cup after Matt Thomson and Joe McBride lifted him shoulder high. From left to right, back row: Charlie Aitken, Peter McCloy, Bobby McCallum, Joe McBride, Pat Delaney, Matt Thomson, John Martis, George Murray.

Four of the first team out training in January 1969. From left to right, they are Willie McCallum, Jackie McInally, John 'Dixie' Deans and Peter McCloy. Willie McCallum, the steady and reliable centre half, was signed by Bobby Ancell from Douglas Water Thistle ten years earlier. Jackie McInally had won a championship medal with Kilmarnock in 1965, while Dixie Deans was later to sign for Jock Stein's Celtic. Peter McCloy, 'The Girvan Lighthouse', signed for Rangers in an exchange deal which saw Bobby Watson and Brian Heron going to Fir Park, and the big goalie heading for Ibrox, where he won every domestic honour and a European Cup Winners Cup medal in 1972.

Ian St. John, manager 1973-1974.

Roger Hynd, manager in the 1978/79 season.

Ally McLeod, manager 1979 to 1981.

Davie Hay, manager in the 1981/82 season.

Willie McLean followed Ian St. John as manager in 1974, and was responsible for establishing Motherwell in the new top ten Premier League which started in the following season. Willie put his hallmark on the team and they became renowned for their uncompromising attitude. Soon, Fir Park was a place where no team wanted to come. His team were also capable of playing attractive football, and with players such as Bobby Graham, Willie Pettigrew, Vic Davidson and Peter Marinello, there was no shortage of skill, finesse and goalscoring ability in his side. Willie Watson, Stuart McLean, Willie McVie and Peter Millar were all players who could win 80/20 challenges, even when these odds were in the opposion's favour. Joe Wark could win the ball without fouling his opponent and Bobby Watson could do a bit of both and still create chances for his front men. Indeed, Willie McLean built a nicely balanced side who finished fourth in the League and reached two Scottish Cup Semi-finals.

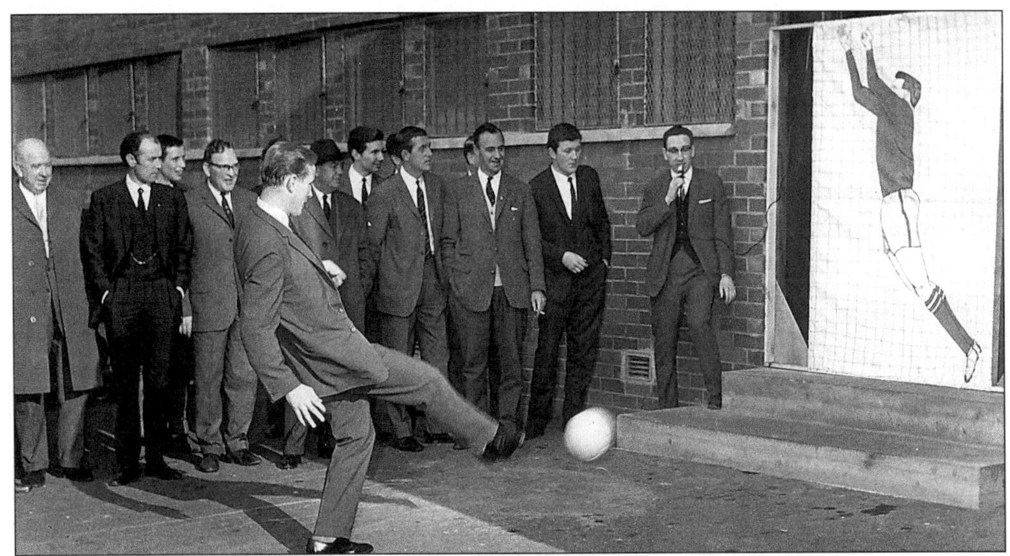

Charlie Aitken officially opens the Fir Park Club. This area is now the Centenary Suite at Fir Park and the Fir Park Club operates from Edward Street. The club moved there and took over the Squash Centre when it became obvious that it was no longer a viable proposition.

The Bobby Howitt team of 1972/73. From left to right, back row: Joe Wark, Davie Whiteford, Billy Ritchie, Bobby Watson, Brain Heron. Middle row: Billy Struthers, Willie McCallum, Jackie McInally, 'Jumbo' Nuir, John Goldthorpe, John Muir, Peter Millar, Tam Forsyth, John French. Front row: Bobby Howitt (Manager), Billy Campbell, Alex Martin, Kirky Lawson, Billy Brown, Jim McCabe, Willie McKenzie (Trainer). It is interesting to note that Billy Brown is currently the assistant manager at Hearts.

Ian St. John returns as manager and is seen here taking the training. 'Sinji' quickly realised the weaknesses in the squad and he signed one of his former Liverpool team-mates, Bobby Graham.

The highly talented Bobby Graham. Bobby turned out to be one of the best players of that decade and his partnership with Willie Pettigrew under McLean became legendary.

1973/74 saw the following squad toe the line at Fir Park. From left to right, back row: Robert McGuiness, William Mills, John French, Keith McRae, Willie Pettigrew, Tom Burns, Davie Main, Alex Ross, John Gray. Middle row: Bobby Watson, Davie Whiteford, John Goldthorpe, 'Jumbo' Muir, Sam Goodwin, Willie McCallum, Kirky Lawson, John Muir. Front row: Willie Leishman, Willie Campbell, Alex Martin, Peter Millar, Joe Wark, Willie McClymont, Jim McCabe, Ian Kennedy.

1974/75 and the biggest changes were the new manager, Ian St. John, and the new jerseys with their distinctive diagonal stripe.

Jimmy O'Rourke follows the ball into the net against Ayr United in this 1977 match at Fir Park.

Peter Marinello (formerly of Hibs, Arsenal and Portsmouth) crosses the ball in this Ayr United match. Ian St. John had moved from Motherwell to Portsmouth, but due to problems (allegedly) Portsmouth could not pay for his transfer. Motherwell were offered Peter Marienello in lieu of a fee and they accepted.

John Grieg is 'debagged' by Gregor Stevens and wriggles into a new pair of shorts. Davie Cooper, Tommy McLean (No. 7) and Gordon Smith of Rangers are also pictured along with Vic Davidson (No.10) of Motherwell.

Andy Lynch of Celtic scores his second own goal of the match past 'keeper Roy Baines. Motherwell won this game 3-2, the other goal being scored by Ian Kennedy.

Bobby Clark of Aberdeen makes a diving save as Marinello and Colin McAdam look on, while Miller awaits the impact. This match was played in the autumn of 1977 at Fir Park. Note the lack of advertising on the perimeter wall.

Penalty! Vic Davidson is pulled down by Davie Robb and Drew Jarvie of Aberdeen. The referee is well placed to give the award.

Gregor Stevens rises above the St Mirren 'keeper Donald Hunter and Tony Fitzpatrick to power home a great goal in this victory over the 'Buddies' in January 1978. Alex Ferguson was the St Mirren manager at the time and he took the defeat rather badly!

Willie Pettigrew scores the winning goal against Celtic in this Scottish Cup match from 1978. Celtic were two goals up at half-time but Willie McLean's pep talk brought about an amazing transformation and the shock result of the round as Celtic left Fir Park with a 3-2 defeat.

The Motherwell line-up for the 1976/77 season. From left to right, back row: Alex Sparks, Jim Ross, Harry Gray, Ian Kennedy, Issac Farrell, Steve Mungall, Jim Lindsay, Mick McManus. Middle row: W. McKenzie (Trainer), Stuart McLaren, Willie Watson, Willie McVie, Ally Hunter, Colin McAdam, Gregor Stevens, Peter Millar, Pat Gardiner, Cliff Barrowman, John Hunter. Front row: Willie McLean (Manager), Jim O'Rourke, Peter Marinello, Vic Davidson, Joe Wark, Bobby Graham, Willie Pettigrew, Craig Brown (Assistant Manager). Craig Brown is now, of course, manager of the Scottish national team.

Roger Hynd took over from Willie McLean and this team picture was taken on 18 January 1978. From left to right, back row: W. Watson, S. Mungall, C. McAdam, W. McVie, H. Gray, G. Stevens, W. Pettigrew, V. Davidson, I. Purdie, Roger Hynd (Manager). Front row: John Haggart (Assistant Manager), I. Kennedy, S. MacLaren, P. Millar, J. Wark, J. O'Rourke, J. Millar, P. Marinello, W. McKenzie (Trainer).

Remember the old Texaco Cup? Here we see Viv Busby of Fulham shooting for goal as Joe Wark, Peter Millar, Willie McVie and Stewart McLaren look on.

The highly successful Fir Park Boys Club in 1977. Iain Ferguson is in the front row, second from the left.

Bobby Watson was signed along with Brian Heron from Rangers in a swap deal that saw Peter McCloy going to Ibrox. Bobby was a very talented wing half and was capped for Scotland against Russia. He later returned to Motherwell as manager in 1983 after a successful spell at Broomfield as manager of Airdrie.

Jimmy O'Rourke was signed by Willie McLean from Hibernian, where he had enjoyed a most successful career. Jimmy was a great player to have in your team and was very popular with the fans.

Keith McCrae was probably the most versatile player ever to play for Motherwell. He was a goalkeeper and yet, in his short time at Fir Park, actually played in every outfield position. Ian St. John sold him to Manchester City in 1974.

Willie McVie was signed from Clyde by Willie McLean. He was a strong and uncompromising centre half and a big favourite with the fans.

Back in 1979, Roger Hynd had won the 'Manager of the Month' award. Motherwell were playing Queens Park in the Scottish Cup at Fir Park on the following Saturday, and prior to the game Roger was duly presented with his award plus a flagon of whisky. The players were then sent out before the match with trays and plastic cups filled with whisky from Roger's bottle to give their fans a 'wee dram'. Unfortunately, Motherwell 'lost their bottle' during the game and the 'jolly old Queens' thrashed them quite comprehensively. A classic case of celebrating too early! Joe Wark is seen here serving the Motherwell fans with their drams.

Chick McLellan, 'Soapy' Soutar and Joe Wark with the mascot. This is a great day for any kid being the mascot on a match day.

Stevie McCleland, who was voted as the 1982 Player of the Year, is hoisted shoulder high by the rest of the squad. Note the seventeen-year-old Gary McAllister (No.34).

Willie Irvine scores against Hamilton Accies, leaving Rikki Ferguson helpless. After leaving Motherwell, 'Noddy' joined Hibs and was to finish as the country's leading goalscorer.

Johnny Gahagan celebrates scoring against Hearts. Johnny was always a great favourite with the Motherwell fans but found it more difficult to please the five different managers for whom he played during his eleven years at Fir Park.

Davie Hay and his players enjoy that winning feeling after clinching promotion to the Premier League in 1982. Can you pick out the young Brian McClair?

The players celebrate after winning the First Division Championship. Among the them are Brian McClair, Alfie Conn, Joe Wark, Brian McLaughlin, Willie Irvine, Ian McLeod, Johnny Gahagan, Stevie McCleland, Brian Coyne, Joe Carson, Iain Clinging, Tommy O'Hara, Bruce Clelland and Graeme Forbes. Assistant manager Jim McFadzean and trainer Willie MacKenzie are also pictured.

Davie Hay (left) and Jim McFadzean, his assistant manager, during the highly successful 1981/82 promotion winning season. Early in August 1981, Ally McLeod resigned as manager at Fir Park after failing to win promotion to the Premier League on three occasions. Ally, to be fair, had inherited an ageing squad. This meant radical changes and players came and went with great rapidity. Without doubt, the most significant move that Ally made was the appointment of Davie Hay as his assistant. Davie's career had been cut short by injury and he was only in his early thirties when he quit Chelsea to join forces with Ally at Fir Park. After Ally resigned, Davie was given temporary control by the Directors, and such was his success that he was given the job on a permanent basis, but only after an agonising wait of over eight weeks. The wisdom of the decision was borne out by a tremendous unbeaten run of 23 games, culminating in the First Division Championship and promotion to the Premier League. They were also the leading goalscorers in Scotland and one of the happiest squads I have ever seen at Fir Park. Sadly, Davie Hay was not too comfortable with the set up at Fir Park, possibly due to the length of time taken by the Directors to appoint him as manager, and opted to work in the USA. He had, however, left Motherwell with a record of success that was second to none, and achieved with only one change to Ally McLeod's squad of players (Tommy O'Hara).

Joe Carson the Motherwell centre half shoots for goal against Rangers at Fir Park. This game was played on 10 December 1982, the anniversary of Motherwell's biggest post war defeat of Rangers at Fir Park. On 10 December 1949, Motherwell beat Rangers 4-0 with goals from McCall (2), Kelly and Watson. It was a really remarkable scoreline against the famous Ibrox 'Iron Curtain.'

The Motherwell squad, 1983/84. From left to right, back row: Jim Burns, Paul McFadden, Nicky Walker, Alex Innes, Ally Maxwell, Hugh Sproat, Robert Shaw, John McStay. Middle row: Jock Wallace (Manager), Mick Cormack, Alex Kennedy, Graeme Forbes, Joe Carson, Johannes Edvaldsson, Ian McLeod, Gary McAllister, Stuart Rafferty. Front row: Bobby Flavell, Ally Mauchlen, Andy Dornan, Joe Wark (Reserve Team Coach), Jim Gillespie, Andy Harrow, John Gahagan.

Six

Tommy McLean 1984-1994

The Motherwell squad, 1984/85. Gary McAllister (back row, second from the left) and Tom Boyd (middle row, fifth from the left) went on to accumulate well over 100 Scottish caps between them.

Raymond Blair, signed from East Fife by Tommy McLean, scores against Clyde on his debut at Fir Park.

Tommy McLean and his squad celebrate winning promotion to the Premier League in the 1984/85 season. The 'Steelmen' have retained their top flight status ever since.

Big Tam Forsyth and Jamie Doyle agree to differ.

Tom Boyd clears the danger in typical fashion in this game against Morton.

John McStay wins promotion for his team with his goal at Firhill against Partick Thistle. Paul McFadden (No. 14) is in close attendance. Years later, when John McStay was playing for Raith Rovers, he was involved in an incident at Ibrox with Duncan Ferguson of Rangers. Ferguson was eventually incarcerated in Barlinnie, but this sad episode did little to help John McStay's playing career with media sympathies being directed elsewhere.

Willie Miller and Charlie Nicholas (No. 7) of Aberdeen look on 'stunned' as Craig Paterson scores for Motherwell. Why do people go to football matches? Just look at the joy on the faces of the 'Well fans to find the answer!

Tommy McLean managed Motherwell from 1984 to 1994, taking the team into the Premier League in his first season in charge and consolidating their top-flight status for the rest of his time in control of the team. Tommy had few equals when it came to picking up players in the transfer market, and subsequently moving them on at a handsome profit. He also instituted a youth policy and his youngsters, aided and abetted by the likes of Davie Cooper, were the backbone of the Scottish Cup winning side of 1991. Tommy moved on to Hearts and briefly to Raith Rovers, before taking charge at Dundee United, from where he resigned early in the 1998/99 season. He brought much needed stability to the club during his time at Motherwell, and his trading in the transfer market made it possible for chairman John Chapman to implement his plans to turn Fir Park into an all-seated stadium.

The mighty Liverpool agreed to play Motherwell at Fir Park to mark the 'Steelmen's' centenary. They sent their strongest squad up to Scotland for this game and there was a capacity crowd on the evening to see how Motherwell would fare against the top team in England. It was a cracking game and Stevie Kirk scored a late goal with a typical header to equalise and take the score to 1-1. The Liverpool squad from that season were from left to right, back row: Mark Lawerenson, Jan Molby, Mike Hooper, Gary Gillespie, Bruce Grobbelar, Kevin McDonald. Middle row: Roy Evans (Trainer), Steve Nicol, Steve McMahon, Jim Beglin, Barry Venison, Paul Walsh, Ronnie Moran (Coach). Front row: Ronnie Whelan, John Wark, Bob Paisley (Team Consultant), Kenny Dalglish (Player/Manager), Alan Hansen (Captain), Craig Johnston, Sammy Lee. I reckon this Liverpool team would walk away with the present English Premiership with ease!

An action shot from the centenary game with Liverpool in 1986. In the frame are Kennedy, Babtie, Gillespie, Nicol, Hansen, Whelan, Kirk and Smith.

Davie Cooper signed for Motherwell in 1989. Tommy McLean bought him from Rangers for a mere £50,000, and this must go down as the steal of the century! More than anyone else, Davie was responsible for Motherwell's Scottish Cup victory in 1991. His presence in the dressing room helped to create the special atmosphere you can only get from a winning team, and Davie, along with Colin O'Neil, set about changing the attitude of the squad until it was such that they felt they were capable of beating anyone. 'Coop' was an established international player when he came to Fir Park and will probably best be remembered in a Scotland jersey for the penalty kick he scored against Wales on the night that Jock Stein died. His Scotland days were now well behind him, although he did get a recall to play against Egypt at Pittodrie in the early 1990s. Many fans believed his arrival at Fir Park was simply to fill in his time, but in my opinion it was at Motherwell that he really blossomed as a player. Gates jumped by over 2,000 as fans flocked to see this talented genius go through his repertoire at every opportunity. The 'Moody Blue' image of his Ibrox days was gone and he 'worked his socks off' every time he pulled on a Claret and Amber jersey. One piece of Cooper magic will stay in my memory forever. Motherwell were playing Celtic and 'Coop' got the ball at the half-way line. He was instantly challenged by Baillie of Celtic and Davie beat him not once but three times before Baillie held up both hands in surrender! Davie relished our Cup victory in 1991, as for the first time he was able to savour the adulation of the fans in an open-topped bus, something that he never experienced at Ibrox. Davie Cooper died in 1995 at the tragically young age of thirty-nine, still playing for his first senior team, Clydebank. The new north stand was nearing completion and by popular demand it was named 'The Davie Cooper Stand.' It was a fitting tribute to one of Scotland's greatest ever football players. On a personal note, I will always miss him, not only as a player, but also as a good friend. When will we see his like again?

The 1991 Scottish Cup winning squad, which battled its way through an epic 4-3 Final and brought the trophy home to Fir Park for the first time in thirty-nine years. From left to right, back row: Iain Ferguson, Nick Cusack, Stevie Kirk, Craig Paterson, Ally Maxwell, Chris McCart, Luc Nijholt. Middle row: Bobby Jenks (Scout), John Philliben, Joe McLeod, Phil O'Donnell, Stevie Bryce, Ian Angus, Jim Griffin, Bobby Holmes (Physio). Front row: Tommy McLean (Manager), Colin O'Neil, Dougie Arnott, Tom Boyd, Jamie Dolan, Davie Cooper, Tom Forsyth (Coach). Sadly, eighteen players couldn't all be selected and Cusack, Bryce, McLeod, Dolan and Philliben were left out. The one who must have hurt more than the others was John Philliben, who had played in all the other games and been a major influence on the team in their drive to the final. For once Tommy McLean let his heart rule his head and gave the nod to Colin O'Neil in preference to John because of his thirty-five yard match winning strike in the semi-final against Celtic. As John Philliben knows, football can be a cruel game at times, and Motherwell would never have won the Cup without 'Softy's' great performances in the earlier rounds.

Below opposite: Sir Stanley Matthews at the House of Commons in 1991 with Mike Watson MP (now Lord Watson) and Ann Taylor. Mike is an 'Arab' and Ann, who opened the Davie Cooper Stand in 1995, is a 'Well fan.

The survivors of the 1952 Scottish Cup victory over Dundee met at Hampden Park on the Wednesday before the 1991 Final as guests of the *Daily Record*. They had won the Scottish Cup by a comfortable 4-0 margin and speculated as to how the result would go this time. From left to right, the veterans are Jimmy Watson (who scored the opening goal in 1952), Andy Paton, Tommy Sloan, Charlie Cox, John Swinburne (who was on the terracing that day), Willie Kilmarnock (Captain of the 1952 winners), and Archie Kelly and Wilson Humphries (both of whom also scored in the 1952 Final). Motherwell's other goal was scored by Willie Redpath. who sadly, along with Johnnie Johnstone, Archie Shaw and Johnnie Aitkenhead, had passed away prior to this reunion. By a strange quirk of fate, Johnnie Johnstone and Willie Redpath died within six hours of one another. Jimmy Watson and Wilson Humphries also both died a few years after this photograph was taken. Andy Paton forecast that Motherwell would win by a convincing margin and he saw many similarties to the wining team of thirty-nine years earlier. It turned out that Andy's confidence was not misplaced.

Tommy McLean and his brother Jim lead out their teams at Hampden on 18 May for the 1991 Scottish Cup Final. Tom Boyd (Motherwell) and Maurice Malpas (Dundee United) were the captains on this momentous day.

Iain Ferguson celebrates scoring the opening goal in the Scottish Cup Final against Dundee United with an unstoppable header from an accurate Jim Griffin cross. Dougie Arnott is elated and Maurice Malpas is shattered.

Luc Nijholt and Davie Cooper celebrate the opening goal scored by Iain Ferguson.

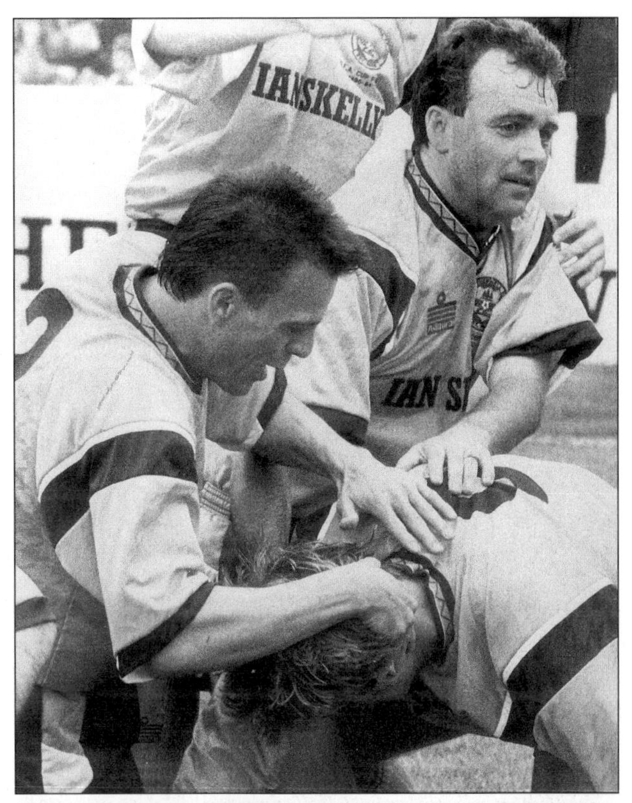

Stevie Kirk heads the ball clear to take some pressure off the Motherwell defence after Craig Patterson collapses from a clash with Miodrag Krivokapic. Mio moved to Motherwell in 1993 and soon became a favourite with the fans. He is currently filling a coaching role at Fir Park.

Young Phil O'Donnell scores Motherwell's second goal in the 1991 Cup Final.

Ian Angus on the point of scoring Motherwell's third goal from the edge of the penalty box.

Stevie Kirk, who found the net in every single round of the Scottish Cup in 1991, salutes the fans after scoring the winning goal in this spectacular 4-3 epic encounter. Luc Nijholt and Dougie Arnott are jubilant.

The terracing erupts as the fans relish 'Kirky's' winning goal.

Cup hero Ally Maxwell holds aloft the Scottish Cup. Within the hour Ally was in hospital and it was touch and go as to whether his burst spleen was removed. Fortunately, they decided not to operate, as otherwise his career would have been over. A real Cup hero!

The team celebrate Motherwell's greatest result in thirty-nine years.

So great was the demand for pre-match meals before the 1991 Cup Final that a marquee was put on the pitch to give us some extra room to feed the masses before Hampden. This was all organised by the VP Club who ran fifteen buses to the Final after food and refreshments. After the victory we all just picked up from where we had left off…

The fans were absolutely delirious and they flooded into Fir Park to welcome the victorious team back to Motherwell. Young and old alike were ecstatic. After thirty-nine long years the Scottish Cup was back at Fir Park!

Left: Davie Cooper heads for the open-topped bus. This was the only time that 'Coop' ever celebrated in this manner and he thought it was fabulous. *Right*: The team leave Fir Park to start their tour of the town.

The bus drives makes its way through a sea of overjoyed 'Well fans.

Andy Paton, Wilson Humphries and Charlie Cox from the 1952 team, along with Jim Griffin, Phil O'Donnell, Luc Nijholt, Colin O'Neil and Chris McCart from the 1991 team, join the Provost and Motherwell Directors as guests of Anderson Longwall. On the extreme right is John 'Darkie' Cummings, the former Hearts wing half.

Iain Ferguson puts pressure on Gary Stevens as Scott Nisbet looks on in this encounter between Motherwell and Rangers at Fir Park. It is worth noting that the 'Well beat Rangers 3-0 just two weeks before their victory in the 1991 Scottish Cup Final.

Bobby Russell scores against Rangers after receiving a defence splitting pass from Davie Cooper, with whom he had that uncanny understanding which occasionally develops between players. Davie and Bobby used this gift to great effect throughout their years together. Here, Gary Stevens and Terry Butcher of Rangers look on helplessly.

Raymond Farningham is seen here in action against Ray 'Butch' Wilkins. Raymond holds the record for emptying Ibrox. In 1987 he scored the only goal of the game with two minutes left to play. Ibrox Stadium was empty within ninety seconds as the totally frustrated 'bluenoses' went home with their tails between their legs. A magic afternoon in the life of a 'Well fan!

Colin O'Neil, Phil O'Donnell and John Philliben celebrate Colin's unforgettable goal in the 1991 Scottish Cup semi-final replay at Hampden. Stevie Kirk had just come onto the park as a substitute and he side-flicked the ball to Colin who was thirty-five yards out from goal (he now claims he was at the halfway line!). Colin looked up and without hesitation screamed the ball into the net past a helpless Pat Bonnar. This took the score to 3-2 in Motherwell's favour, and Stevie Kirk, as usual, added a fourth. Wee Dougie Arnott had scored both Motherwell's other goals. This goal earned Colin his appearance in the final and, later, a testimonial match when his career was tragically cut short by injury. Colin is one of football's great characters and there was a classic case when he elbowed Peter Grant of Celtic in the mouth after an off-the-ball incident. Colin waited until the referee was otherwise occupied and whacked Peter as he ran past. 'Honest, John,' he said to me, 'not a soul was watching and I was only getting a wee bit of my own back. It was worth it even though I needed an operation after the game to remove Peter's teeth from my elbow!' What Colin failed to realise was that millions saw him fouling Peter on television, including those in authority. He received a six-match ban, which was attributed to a report from the supervisor in the stand and not television evidence.

Tommy Coyne holds the record as Motherwell's most capped player. He was honoured thirteen times for his country while he was a 'Well player, but unfortunately for Scotland his caps were for the Irish Republic. This is a typical shot of Tommy, with Andy Goram (then of Rangers) diving at his feet. Tommy is held in the highest esteem by Motherwell fans and is currently playing for Dundee. In his career he has scored goals for Clydebank, Dundee United, Dundee, Celtic, Tranmere Rovers, Motherwell and now once again for Dundee. He is a very cultured player and an excellent professional.

Miodrag Krivokapic in action against Charlie Miller of Rangers. Mio was signed by Tommy McLean in 1993 from Dundee United, who had bought him from Red Star Belgrade where he had won twenty-five caps for his country. Mio brought a new standard of defensive play to Motherwell and the fans are delighted that he has returned to Fir Park in a coaching capacity. He scored a marvellous goal at Easter Road which has become part of the club's folklore. A highly respected player and a really nice guy.

Tommy McLean brought together a star-studded team of guest players to play Motherwell in the John Gahagan benefit match. From left to right, back row: Tom McAdam, Paul Smith, Joe Tortillano, Ally McCoist, Nicky Walker, John Brown, Keith Wright, Gary McAllister, Gordon Hunter, Ally Mauchlen. Front row: Freddy van der Hoorn, Andy Walker, Stuart Rafferty, Billy McKinlay, Fraser Wishart.

The cost of rebuilding Fir Park was partially offset by a Motherwell Football Club Development Committee who raised funds by various methods to assist the club with its burden. Here are the Committee handing over a cheque for £10,000 in October 1992. From left to right: John Swinburne, Steve Morgan, Bill Crawford, Jamie Chapman, Allan Dick, Peter Callan and Martin Rose.

Brian Martin was signed by Tommy McLean in the season after Motherwell won the Scottish Cup. He was always a great favourite with the fans and should have received greater recognition from his country. A stalwart central defender, he coped with opponents with ease, and the bigger the name the better Brian played.

Seven

McLeish and Kampman 1994-1998

A typical McLeish squad. The season before Alex McLeish took over as manager, Tommy McLean took Motherwell into third place in the Premier League. With virtually the same squad Alex McLeish reached second place in the League. If only Sieb Dykstra had not been sold to QPR and Phil O'Donnell to Celtic, then I believe that Motherwell could have gone all the way and emulated the great achievement of 'Sailor' Hunter in 1931/32. During his time at Motherwell, Alex spent in the vicinity of £2.5 million on new players and took his team from second to the nether regions of the Premier League, where they were constantly engaged in relegation battles. He left a few days before our Cup game with Rangers to go to Hibs, but failed to keep them in the top ten. After a poor start Hibs went on an excellent run, gaining promotion to the SPL in 1998/99.

Mickey Weir in action against Celtic in 1997. Mickey scored the winning goal in a memorable 2-1 victory.

'Big Eck' clowns about with Colin O'Neil and Jamie Dolan before Colin's testimonial game against Ipswich Town.

Malky McCormack produced this cartoon for the Motherwell match programme after 'Big Eck's' team had gone more than nine games without scoring a single goal. It shows Alex McLeish giving his forwards a tactics talk on how to score goals.

Dougie Arnott, who was one of the most whole-hearted players to pull on a Motherwell jersey, is seen here celebrating yet another goal. During his eleven years with Motherwell he scored 23 goals against the Old Firm and only played twice in a losing side against Celtic. No wonder the 'Well fans worshipped him! His two goals against Celtic in the Semi-final replay were pivotal in taking the team through to the 1991 Scottish Cup Final.

Tommy Coyne in action against Borussia Dortmund with the unfinished Davie Cooper Stand in the background.

In the final league match of the 1996/97 season, Motherwell needed to win to avoid the dreaded drop. With about ten minutes left for play, Mitchell van der Gaag unleashed an unstoppable volley from all of forty yards to give Motherwell three points and save the club from relegation. Mitchell van der Gaag never played for Motherwell again, returning to Holland to sign for Utrecht. Peter Muss, who owns Equibrite, has this photograph proudly hanging in his office.

Ian Adams and various other members of the President's Club at Fir Park present club chairman John Chapman with Willie Kilmarnock's cup winner's medal and framed photograph. Ian Adams raised the money from his colleagues and purchased the medal at Christie's auction in Glasgow.

A view of Fir Park before chairman John Chapman set about rebuilding the whole ground to comply with the full requirements of the Taylor Report. John Chapman came to a club in crisis in late December 1981. He was largely responsible for eliminating the £1 million burden of debt and for his last nine years as chairman the club was always 'in the black.' He is generally regarded as the saviour of the club.

A determined Lee McCulloch in action against Joachim Bjorklund of Rangers.

The Committee for the Jim Griffin Benefit Year. From left to right, back row: Martin H. Rose, Ricky Jordan and Robert Nimmo. Front row: Bill Beatie, Tony Joyce and Bill Crawford.

The floodlighting pylons come down from the south terracing in 1992 and work is underway as Motherwell start to comply with the findings of the Taylor Report.

The late Andy Russell surveys the scene with a quiet smile to himself. He knows that he will no longer be required to clean that terracing again!

The solid foundations are laid for the massive structure that was to arise from here.

The new pylons are delivered and the structural work goes on apace.

The main cross beam, which is around seventy-five metres long, is dropped into place. It was only about one-eighth of an inch out. The structural work was carried out locally by Bone, Connell and Baxter Ltd.

The steel structure continues to grow.

The roof on the Motorola Stand nears completion.

The Motorola Stand is completed and ready to receive the away fans. It was filled to capacity on the first occasion that it was opened in a game against Rangers in January 1993.

The old North Terracing pie stall was a favourite meeting place for fans. Before segregation it was possible to meet here and go around the other end if Motherwell were kicking that way.

The framework goes up in the Davie Cooper stand. Note the advertising around. This was prior to the match against Dortmund in September 1994.

A fantastic aerial view of the completed Fir Park.

Stevie McMillan is a young player with a huge future ahead of him provided he steers clear of injuries. Already an Under-21 internationalist, it will not be long before he is a regular in the Scotland squad if he continues to make progress. Stevie has a tremendous left foot and his speed was clocked at 69 mph in a penalty competition organised by Mitre at Fir Park.

Harri Kampman was brought over from Finland to manage Motherwell when 'Big Eck' left to go to Hibs. He adopted a style which was too negative for the fans and despite keeping our place in the top ten, the results were not good enough. In October 1998, Harri opted to return to his native Finland, thus ending his brief spell as manager. Although Bobby Watson was manager at Fir Park for a shorter period of time, he was in control of more games. Harri's time took in the close season, while Bobby Watson took over in October 1983 and left in May 1984.

Eight

New Motherwell Into the New Millennium: John Boyle and Billy Davies

Billy Davies, the youngest ever manager of Motherwell Football Club. His approach to the tactical side of the game is like a breath of fresh air in the restrictive environment of the Scottish Premier League. Entertainment is his top priority and the fans really enjoy his attitude.

John Spencer was the first player signed by Billy Davies. At that time Motherwell were adrift at the bottom of the League with a mere nine points. 'Spenny' scored the only goal of the game on his debut against Rangers. A great start to his Motherwell career!

These Motherwell fans get everywhere. Here is Danny Greenberg from Edinburgh at the Maracana Stadium, posing in his favourite Motherwell tee-shirt.

The World Cup and yes, Motherwell are represented once again. Alan Swinburne, a member of the Tartan Army, is in full war paint with his Motherwell top at the Stade de France.

Chairman John Boyle with Pat Nevin after Pat had signed up at Motherwell. John and Pat have been friends for years and they both have a vision for Motherwell which will transform the club as it heads into the new millennium.

As soon as Motherwell signed him from Kilmarnock, Pat Nevin was appointed chief executive at Fir Park. Although he is still very much a player, Pat is in the unique position of being the first player/chief executive in Scottish Football. Indeed, John Boyle also wanted to make Pat a director of the club, but unfortunately the archaic rules of the SFA prevented this from officially taking place. It is simply a matter of time, however, before Pat is appointed to the board at Motherwell. As a player, Pat has played at the very highest level of the game in a career that began at Clyde, before subsequent moves to Chelsea, Everton, Tranmere Rovers and Kilmarnock. Capped by Scotland, he is a winger in the traditional mode – very skilful with great vision, the ability to cross the ball accurately and, of course, a great eye for goal.

Steven Nicholas is seen here making his debut against Aberdeen. The young seventeen-year-old has the world at his feet if he works hard at his game and avoids injuries. Billy Davies signed him from Stirling Albion, managed by that old Motherwell favourite John Philliben. With talent like this available, the future of our game is looking good!

Shaun Teale, the popular central defender. A great favourite with the 'Well fans.

Andy Goram was signed by Billy Davies in January 1999. Andy played for Scotland on forty-two occasions and won every domestic honour available to him. There is no doubt that Andy Goram is the finest goalkeeper Scotland has produced for decades and it was a most ambitious move to bring him to Fir Park.

Ged Brannan signed for Motherwell on the same day that John Spencer arrived. A cultured midfield player with a tremendous shot, Ged has been a great acquisition.

Michel Doesburg was one of a Dutch contingent of players who came to Motherwell at the beginning of the 1998/99 season. Michel was an instant hit with the fans and he proved to be a most diligent defender in the Luc Nijholt mould. He actually played in the same team as Luc when he started out on his career in Holland.

Motherwell experimented for the first time with a hot air balloon over the playing surface in 1999. This was over thirty feet high and had the added advantage that players could train on the grass despite the hard frost outside. This photograph by Jim Donnelly gives some idea of the size of this hot air balloon.

Little did Billy Davies imagine as he posed for this pre-season photograph that by October he would find himself being appointed as manager of Motherwell Football Club. Despite being only thirty-four years of age, Billy has taken to the job like a duck takes to water. He has applied simple principles and by treating players in the manner that he always respected as a player he has won over the squad and the fans. John Boyle and Pat Nevin have given Billy complete backing and some of his signings have really captured the imagination of the supporters who for far too long have seen great players leave Fir Park in order to balance the books. Even more important is the fact that Billy Davies has nailed his colours to the mast and opted for open, attacking and attractive football. All this is guaranteed to bring the fans flooding back to Fir Park, especially when allied to John Boyle's long-sighted pricing initiatives.

The new owner of Motherwell Football Club, John Boyle, has made a huge impact at Fir Park. The fans were instantly won over by his enlightened policy for admission prices at the ground, and for the first time in decades the sights have been raised when it comes to targeting players to strengthen our squad. Who would have thought that Motherwell would have brought talented players such as Andy Goram, Ged Brannan, Pat Nevin and John Spencer to Fir Park? Watch this space.

Stevie Kirk, who did more than most to make 1991 a memorable season. Stevie scored in every round of the Scottish Cup and as far as the majority of Motherwell fans are concerned, he is a legend.